I0605817

the little book of MOON MAGIC

First published in 2026 by OH
An Imprint of HEADLINE PUBLISHING GROUP LIMITED

1

Disclaimer:
This book is intended for general informational purposes only and should not be relied upon as recommending or promoting any specific practice, diet or method of treatment. It is not intended to diagnose, advise, treat or prevent any illness or condition and is not a substitute for advice from a professional practitioner of the subject matter contained in this book. You should not use the information in this book as a substitute for medication, nutritional, diet, spiritual or other treatment that is prescribed by your practitioner. Furthermore, the publisher is not affiliated with and does not sponsor or endorse any uses of or beliefs about in any way referred in this book.

Cataloguing in Publication Data is available from the British Library

ISBN 978-1-03543-333-9

Compiled and written by Katalin Németh
Editorial: Phoebe Hills
Designed and typeset in Joanna Sans Nova by Andy Jones
Project manager: Russell Porter
Illustrations: Freepik.com
Production: Arlene Lestrade
Printed and bound in Dubai

Headline's policy is to use papers that are natural, renewable and recyclable products and made from wood grown in well-managed forests and other controlled sources. The logging and manufacturing processes are expected to conform to the environmental regulations of the country of origin.

HEADLINE PUBLISHING GROUP LIMITED
An Hachette UK Company
Carmelite House, 50 Victoria Embankment, London EC4Y 0DZ

The authorised representative in the EEA is Hachette Ireland, 8 Castlecourt Centre, Dublin 15, D15 XTP3, Ireland (email: info@hbgi.ie)

www.headline.co.uk www.hachette.co.uk

the little book of

MOON MAGIC

katalin németh

CONTENTS

CHAPTER 1

INTRODUCTION

Inspirer of artists, lovers and witches alike, the Moon has always been one of the most important heavenly bodies, second only to the Sun.

The Moon influences the tides, the seasons, animals' procreation and their navigation at night, how plants grow; it affects nearly everything in our lives, even our planet's orbit.

It plays a prominent role in the arts and media as well. Even if you aren't a movie buff, you will probably have heard of *The Trip to the Moon*, which was the very first science fiction movie ever made, in 1902.

Since then, countless moon-inspired movies, cartoons and series have been made. Think of *Pretty Guardian Sailor Moon*, the trendsetting series in the “magical girl” manga and anime subgenre; the songs that use the Moon as a metaphor for feelings towards a romantic partner; and poems likening the face of the poet’s beloved to that of the Moon.

Every culture has unique lore related to the Moon.

The Japanese book *The Tale of the Bamboo Cutter*, who finds a moon princess in a bamboo shoot; the story of Chang'e, the Chinese moon goddess after whom the country's rockets are named; the Hindu myth of how the moon god Chandra was cursed for favouring one of his 27 wives; the Norse myth of Hjúki and Bil, the children stolen by Máni – the Moon personified.

Our fascination with the Moon has given birth to many tales and beliefs, along with very real observations and magical practices involving this celestial body.

Studies have found that moon-based agriculture brings better results. It is an established belief, now supported by a growing volume of scientific evidence, that sowing seeds during the moon's waxing phase encourages better crops and weeding in the waning phase delays their regrowth.

The Moon plays a central role in astrology – whichever zodiac sign the Moon is in at your time of birth will determine your inner world, emotional self and subconscious desires.

And, of course, we cannot forget witchcraft. Dancing naked under the full moon may not be a widespread practice, but witches all over the world channel the power of the Moon in their spells and look for protection and wisdom from our beautiful satellite.

Whether you are a practitioner of magic or simply want to harness the Moon's energy in a more tangible way, I hope you find something useful and new in this book.

Blessings
on your journey!

CHAPTER 2

MAGICAL MOON

CREATING the MOON ALTAR

The Moon has always had a central place in witchcraft, its gentle light and protective energy overseeing many a witch's work.

A moon altar is a sacred space that encourages a deeper connection with the moon when conducting rituals, allowing you to better draw on its magical energy and powers.

In this chapter, we will discuss how you can integrate the Moon into your practice, starting with creating an altar to enhance your witchcraft.

Creating an altar doesn't have to be difficult or expensive. An altar can be anything you want it to be, from a piece of rock on a shelf to a whole room filled with moon stone. The choice is yours.

The main thing to consider is whether the space reminds you of the Moon and its energy and if it feels magical to you – after all, you're the one who will work your magic at it.

Choose a space for your altar that will not be in the way or disturbed by others, including children or pets. It could be a bedside table, a shelf on your book case or the inside of a drawer.

Cleanse and consecrate the surface by wiping it clean then sprinkling moon water on it. Establish your intention clearly: you are making this space sacred and magical.

Spread your altar cloth on the surface, then place your sacred items on top of it.

What you put on your altar is up to you. You could consider having statues of moon deities, depictions of the phases of the Moon, crystals, herbs and flowers, your moon journal or spell book, moon water and your magical work tools, such as your athame, incense, candles and so on.

It all depends on personal preference and any traditions you may belong to.

If you don't have the opportunity to openly display your sacred space, look into pocket or travel altars on the internet. You will be amazed what you can do with a matchbox or a small jewellery box.

Remember, it's never the size of the altar that matters in witchcraft, but your intention.

MOON WATER and ECLIPSE WATER

Moon water is used in many rituals and spells, and is generally good to have on your altar, just in case you have an urgent spell to do.

MOON WATER

To create moon water, first set your intention and choose the corresponding moon phase.

If you want generic moon water that can enhance any intention, choose a **full moon** night to make it.

Moon water stays potent for about a month, so you will need to make a new batch every **full moon**. You can use older moon water, but it might not be as efficient.

Pouring leftover moon water onto plants is a great way to dispose of it, because the plants will still benefit from any leftover energy.

Buy a clear glass bottle that you will exclusively use for moon water. It should be completely see through, so it lets the Moon's energy through. If you don't have the means to buy glass, then see-through plastic bottles are also acceptable.

Fill this bottle with clean water. You can use store-bought bottled water, use a water filter, or boil tap water to get rid of as many of its impurities as possible. If you boil your water, let it cool down before you pour it into the bottle.

Place the bottle somewhere where it will get direct moonlight – either on a windowsill or in your garden. The water will still absorb the Moon's energy if it is cloudy outside, although it may not be as potent.

Put it there after sunset, leave it out for the night and bring it inside before sunrise. Store the bottle in a dark place to preserve its energy.

You can use moon water for ritual baths, for cleansing your spaces and tools, for anointing your tools, as a base for potions, and to drink before rituals for heightened magical energy and intuition.

If you plan to drink it, make sure it is safe to do so.

ECLIPSE WATER

Making eclipse water follows the same process but during the night of an eclipse.

Remember it is doubly potent, but has a very chaotic and disruptive energy, so it is best suited for banishing spells.

Definitely not for manifestation work.

PERIOD MAGIC

This wouldn't be a lunar magic book if we didn't mention using period blood in your practice.

While it isn't talked about much as the subject is considered to be taboo, using your blood if you menstruate can supercharge your spells.

Menstrual blood is best suited for banishing spells and letting things go, but it can also be used to consecrate your tools and make them deeply yours, too.

Some interesting trivia: in folk magic, period blood was used in love spells. A witch would bake it into scones that were then fed to the chosen victim, who would supposedly fall head over heels for her.

moon related DIVINATION SPREADS

If you practice any kind of divination, you know how valuable it is to do regular tarot readings for yourself to track your progress over time.

Divination spreads, or tarot spreads, provide a framework for these readings, allowing you to interpret the cards based on the question or area into which you are seeking insight.

There are a plethora of moon-related spreads online you can try, or you could make up your own. By using the phases of the Moon you can enhance your readings and better connect with your own intuition and lunar energy.

You can relate the card positions in the spread to the phases of the Moon, to the zodiac sign the Moon is in at the time of the reading, or to a moon deity you'd like to work with.

An example of a divination spread could be using the aspects of the triple goddess. Give this a go and track your answers over a year, see where your journey is heading.

Don't worry if you have similar cards or runes every time you do the spread. This just means you are still working on the same lesson or task.

the TRIPLE GODDESS DIVINATION SPREAD

Position one, the Maiden:

What is something new I need to bring into my life?

Position two, the Mother:

What is something I need to nurture in my life?

Position three, the Crone:

What is something I need to learn in my life?

tables of CORRESPON-DENCES

Tables of Correspondences are lists of magical relationships between different elements. Using these items together in rituals can help you select the right tools and make the effects more powerful.

There are many elements across different realms that correspond with the Moon, from spritital deities to earthly plants and scents. Include these in your moon altar and spells to harness potent lunar energy.

GODS and GODDESSES ASSOCIATED with the MOON

gods: Khonsu, Mani, Chandra, Shiva, Avatea, Arma, Mēn, Tarqiup Inua, Abaangui, Bahloo.

goddesses: Selene, Artemis, Hecate, Arianrhod, Freya, Isis, Yemaya, Nanna, Mama Killa, Kuutar, Ix Chel, Auchimalgen, Tonantzin, Alignak.

CRYSTALS ASSOCIATED with the MOON

Moonstone, clear quartz, labradorite, amethyst, selenite, lapis lazuli.

PLANTS ASSOCIATED with the MOON

Moonflower, gardenia, mugwort, jasmine; any white or silver coloured flower and flowers that bloom at night, plants that enhance psychic abilities.

SCENTS ASSOCIATED with the MOON

Jasmine, sandal wood, rose, myrrh, lavender, gardenia.

CHAPTER 3

MOON PHASES

The Moon reflects light that it receives from the Sun. As it circles the Earth, rays of sunlight strike its surface and illuminate different portions of its face.

Let us now explore how we can harness this celestial power and transform into the best version of ourselves we can be!

sun
earth

the PHASES of the MOON

Timing your magical workings to the Moon's phases and its place in the zodiac signs will give extra power to your spells and rituals.

Using the information below, plan your practice accordingly and see how much easier your spell will come to fruition.

the first phase

the NEW MOON

This is the phase when the Moon is not illuminated by the Sun and is barely visible in the sky.

It lasts one to three nights.

The **new moon** is the best time for new beginnings, releasing what doesn't serve you and banishing spells.

the second phase

WAXING CRESCENT

This is the phase when the Moon looks like a crescent that will grow into the letter D.

It lasts for about six nights.

The **waxing crescent** is the time for goal setting, self-care and rejuvenation.

the third phase

the FIRST QUARTER

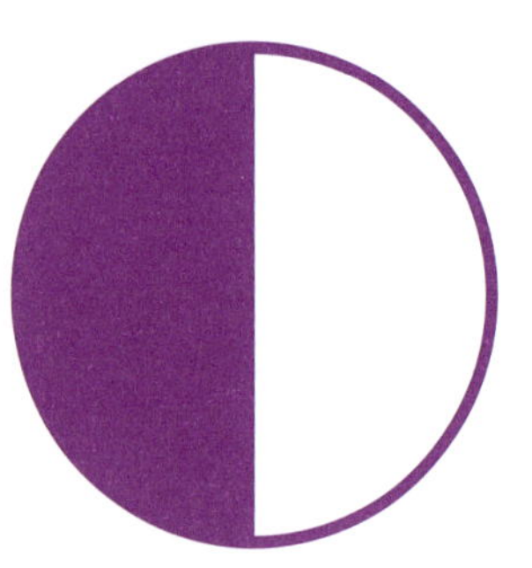

This is the phase when the Moon looks like the letter D.

It lasts one night.

The **first quarter** is the time to take the first steps towards your dreams and for motivational spells.

the fourth phase

WAXING GIBBOUS

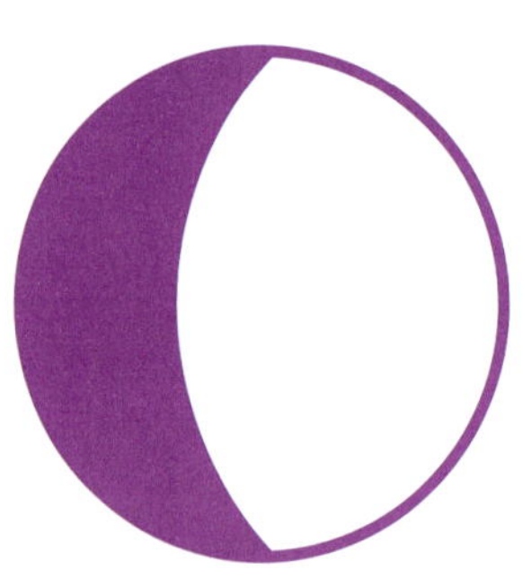

This is the phase when the Moon looks like something between the letters D and O; almost full.

It lasts for about six nights.

waxing gibbous is the time to re-adjust your plans, take stock and evaluate your life.

the fifth phase

FULL MOON

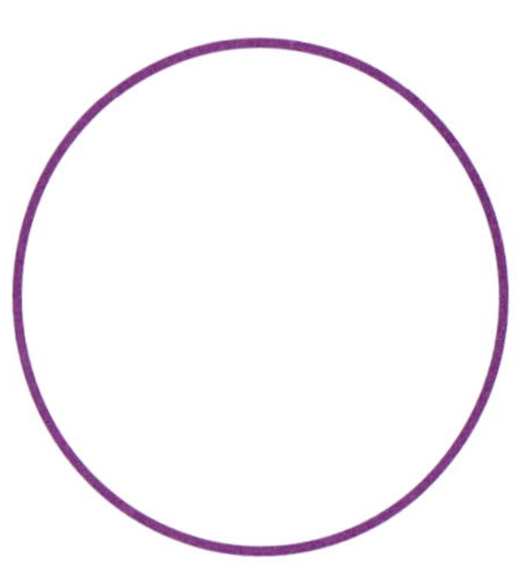

This is the phase when the Moon is a complete circle in the sky, fully illuminated by the Sun.

It lasts one night.

A **full moon** is the best time for celebrating, making your project public, making moon water, manifestation spells and psychic development.

the sixth phase

WANING GIBBOUS

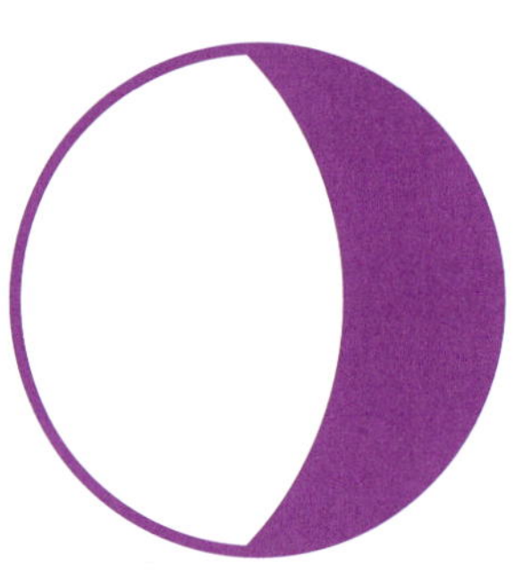

This is the phase when the Moon starts to disappear, and from an O it slowly becomes a C.

It lasts for about six nights.

waning gibbous is the best time for closure, moving forward, learning lessons and charitable work

the seventh phase

the THIRD QUARTER

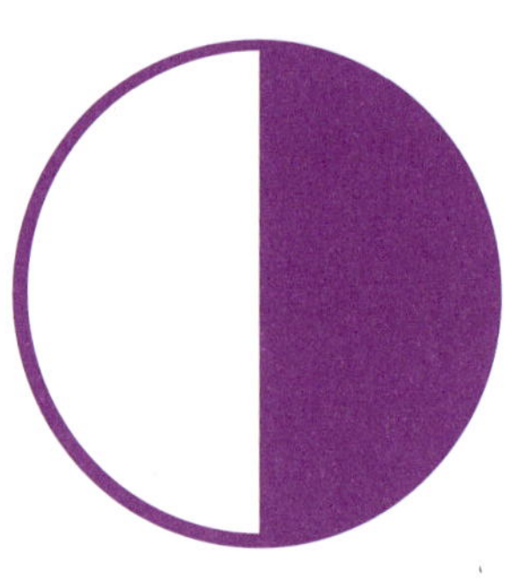

This is the phase when the Moon looks like a flipped-over letter D.

It lasts one night.

The **third quarter** is a time for forgiveness, healing from trauma and reconnecting to your higher self.

the eighth phase

WANING CRESCENT

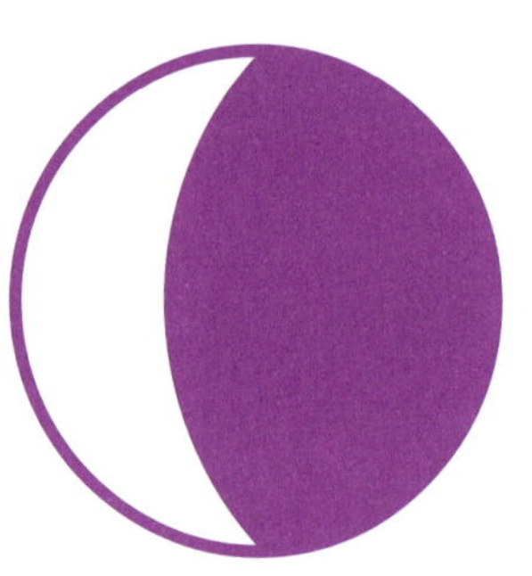

This is the phase when the Moon looks like a letter C.

It lasts for about six nights.

The **waning crescent** is the best time for releasing the past, surrendering to the Universe and for recuperation.

the fifth phase

BLUE MOON

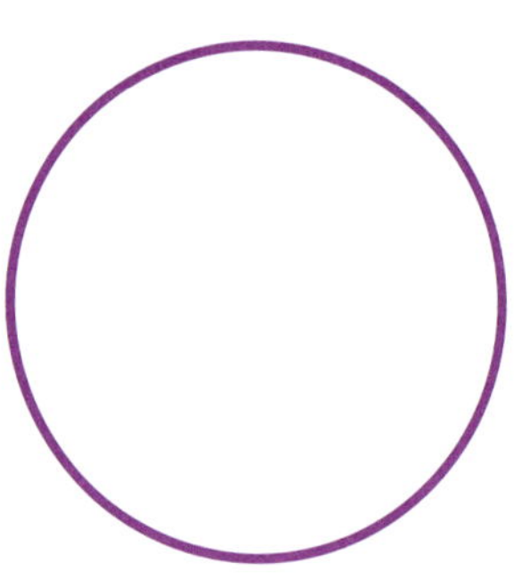

When there are two full moons within one calendar month, the second is called a blue moon.

It acts as an amplified full moon and is perfect for manifestation and psychic development.

A **blue moon** supercharges spells and moon water.

the first phase

the LUNAR ECLIPSE

When on the night of a **full moon** the Earth passes between the Moon and the Sun, temporarily thrusting the Moon into darkness, a lunar eclipse occurs.

It brings endings and transformations into our lives and has a powerful, but unpredictable and disruptive energy.

Although its energy will supercharge any spell you do, it's better not to risk the eclipse's chaotic energy wreaking havoc in your life.

CHAPTER 4

MOON SIGNS in ASTROLOGY

Even people who aren't interested in astrology will probably know their sun sign or "birth sign". This is the sign most commonly referred to when talking about horoscopes, and is easy to find out because the Sun spends roughly a month in each zodiac sign.

Calculating your Moon sign is a little more complicated, because the Moon only spends two and a quarter days in each sign, and it passes through the entire zodiac cycle in about a month.

In addition, where you are in the world will also influence your Moon sign: a person born in Europe may have a different sign to someone born in Australia, even if they were born at exactly the same time.

This is why it is important to know the exact location, date and time of our birth, at least to the hour; if you were born on a day when the Moon transitioned from one sign to another, it could be the specific hour and minute that determines your sign.

This is also how auspicious times – specific periods that are considered good for starting important activities – are calculated, for example in Vedic astrology.

They consider the exact position of the Moon in the sky as well as the horoscopes of the relevant people, and pinpoint a short window when a certain activity – like a marriage or a special ritual – can take place.

The Moon signs show how we really are, as opposed to the Sun signs that reflect how we behave in and influence the world.

The Moon reveals our true nature, our strengths and weaknesses, likes and dislikes and things we need to be mindful of.

the MOON in ARIES

Aries Moons are born leaders, loving independence and exploration. They are mentally brave and strong, and use this quality to embark on sometimes risky adventures. In their formative years they can be quite rebellious and need to learn early on how to direct their energy towards positive, constructive things instead of self-destructive ones.

They love sports and are very competitive. They are the kind of person who finds extreme sports relaxing and need physical activity in their lives.

They will work hard for their dreams and they have the capacity to make them into reality.

They express their feelings freely, but need to learn how to do this without hurting others, or themselves. They can sometimes expect too much too soon from others.

Aries Moons fall in love easily and will pursue their love interest relentlessly. It is important to teach them early on about coercion and consent.

For them to have a successful relationship, they need an equally strong partner who is just as loyal, passionate and adventurous as they are.

They are most compatible with Leo and Aquarius Moons.

The Moon in Aries is the best time for magical workings involving new beginnings, starting a business and conflict resolution.

the MOON in TAURUS

Taurus Moons are practical and careful, who love safety and stability. They are wise beyond their years, which makes them easy to raise as children.

They can find common ground with anyone and are patient when listening to the other person talk, meaning they can often be a family favourite, especially with grandparents. They are dependable, know what they want and will work tirelessly to achieve it.

That said, Taurus Moons will avoid taking risks where they can and dislike change, however small it is. Stability is their life goal.

They enjoy relaxing activities: meditation, arts and crafts, reading – they like to feel safe and unrushed, especially in their down time.

They don't rush into relationships and prefer long-term romance over passionate but short-lived flames.

They are hard to seduce, but once they feel comfortable enough to love someone, they will protect that person and relationship with their life.

They are most compatible with Cancer, Pisces, Capricorn and fellow Taurus Moons.

The Moon in Taurus is the best time for magical workings involving love, fertility, gardening, commitments, buying or renovating the house and money-related spells.

the MOON in GEMINI

Gemini Moons are curious, intelligent, adaptable and forever young. They have an immutable thirst for knowledge; they need to know how everything works.

They usually start speaking at an early age and their first word might very well be "why?". In their downtime, they enjoy reading and researching.

Gemini Moons love gadgets and will buy the latest ones, especially if it means menial tasks get lifted off their shoulders.

They stay up-to-date with trends, they know the current slang and do their best to stay hip.

At the same time, they can sometimes be a bit disorganised, which is where their gadgets can come in handy.

They need their freedom to explore the world and can't suffer jealousy and clinginess in a partner.

They might struggle with commitment and expressing their feelings, even though they are otherwise very communicative. If they find a partner with similar values, it can work wonderfully between them.

They are most compatible with Leo, Libra and Aquarius Moons.

The Moon in Gemini is the best time for magical workings involving business (see page 166), travel, self-identity and creative writing.

the MOON in CANCER

Cancer Moons are emotional and empathetic – they listen to their heart above all else. They have a strong sense of justice and can't watch others suffer. They need and enjoy their family's stability and love, and feel best at home.

They are the kind of children who love playing with dolls and adore taking care of their siblings. They will behave in this way with their partner and children, too. They are natural nurturers, who find pleasure in ding domestic tasks like baking and cooking for their family.

Cancer Moons are well suited to teaching and nursing jobs.

They are often empaths and need to learn how to ground themselves and not take on other people's moods and illnesses. They also need to learn that not everyone is worthy of their limitless giving nature; that there are people who will exploit it.

It's important for Cancer Moons to know their own boundless strength, realise their worth and set firm boundaries before they completely exhaust themselves in service to others.

In a relationship, they need an equally mature and nurturing partner to refill their reserves.

They are most compatible with Taurus, Virgo, Pisces and fellow Cancer Moons.

The Moon in Cancer is the best time for magical workings involving nurturing relationships, family, home, love, intuition, healing and forgiveness.

the MOON in LEO

Leo Moons are self-assured and magnetic, who adore the limelight. They are born entertainers and love to be the centre of attention, which can sometimes make their behaviour over the top, especially as children.

They feel neglected if they are not seen and praised, and require constant validation. They benefit from learning early on that their worth isn't dependent on their performative achievements or other people's praise – and they shouldn't value others in this way either.

Leo Moons love living luxuriously and showing off their wealth. This may cause financial problems as they are prone to overspend. They are great at networking and enjoy climbing the hierarchical ladder to the top.

They can be wonderful, charming leaders, both at work and in their relationships, as long as people submit to their will. In their romantic life, they are generous and loving, and can be very caring as long as they receive what they want from their partner.

If their partner can set firm boundaries and stick to them, the Leo Moon can be an amazing spouse.

They are most compatible with Aries, Gemini and Sagittarius Moons.

The Moon in Leo is the best time for magical workings involving self-confidence, self-expression, performing arts, leadership and networking.

the MOON in VIRGO

Virgo Moons are practical, calm, logical and serious. They are great at planning ahead and face all obstacles with a quiet resolve and dignity.

They might be shy as children and highly introverted as they grow up; they need to learn how to express themselves and not internalise everything.

Sometimes they can really overthink things and worry about what others might think, meaning they miss out on all the fun.

Virgo Moons are proud perfectionists and expect the same from everyone else. They have a deep respect for sharp intellect and don't let their feelings control them.

They can be content alone, they don't need a partner to feel complete. If they decide to look for someone, they are great at analysing their prospective significant other, and will only express their feelings once they are comfortable in the relationship.

They are most compatible with Taurus, Cancer and Capricorn Moons.

The Moon in Virgo is the best time for magical workings involving self-discipline, intelligence, work-relationships, cleansing, healing and service to others.

the MOON in LIBRA

Libra Moons are charming and friendly with everyone they meet. They have a strong sense of integrity and are tactful and diplomatic.

They believe in doing thorough research into everything, which might make them seem unconfident, but they just like to have all the available information before making up their mind.

Libra Moons crave peace, which might make them people pleasers. This is one of the main things they need to learn in life: no matter what they do, there will always be people who don't like them, which is why setting boundaries and having clear values are so important.

Those that dislike them will be in minority, however, because of the Libra Moon's natural charm and adaptability.

They require their partner to be somewhat old-fashioned and gentle in order to feel safe and loved.

They are most compatible with Taurus, Gemini and Aquarius Moons.

The Moon in Libra is the best time for magical workings involving legal proceedings, finding balance and partnerships in both your personal and business life.

the MOON in SCORPIO

Scorpio Moons are magnetic, mysterious, razor sharp and intense. They know their worth and aren't afraid to use their skill and charm to get what they want.

They have focus and drive, meaning they can become extremely successful. They thrive as leaders and people like working for them.

They command discipline and respect but lead with empathy. They need to learn to let go of wanting to control everything and everyone at all times.

Scorpio Moons have a complex, often turbulent, inner life, but they are masters of hiding their emotions. Maybe because of this, they find it easy to see through lies and manipulation and they don't put up with it.

It's extremely rare that they'd give a second chance to anyone – "fool me once", they say.

Many of them have psychic abilities and they are often fascinated by death from a young age.

They can be passionate lovers, with sex often being the top priority in their romantic relationships.

They are most compatible with Cancer, Leo and Pisces Moons.

The Moon in Scorpio is the best time for magical workings involving sex, death, psychic gifts, magic and transformation, unveiling secrets, and the truth. It is also a good time for business (see page 166).

the MOON in SAGITTARIUS

Sagittarius Moons are open minded and curious – indomitable free spirits.

They live for adventure and are always on the move, ready to try out anything new.

While their boundless energy is admirable, sometimes they can get into trouble for making a split-second decision without any thinking, so they need to learn to be a little more deliberate.

Sagittarius Moons can be brutally honest and involuntarily come across as imprudent. They need to learn boundaries and tact, especially when it comes to interactions with the general public.

They are joyful, bubbly people with a good sense of humour and a positive outlook on life.

They love getting together with their friends and loved ones, and don't need a romantic partner to feel happy.

If they date, they need an equally confident free spirit, who understands them and isn't a jealous, clingy type.

They are most compatible with Aries, Gemini, Leo and fellow Sagittarius Moons.

The Moon in Sagittarius is the best time for magical workings involving adventures, fun, joy, education, resilience and travel.

the MOON in CAPRICORN

Capricorn Moons are careful, mature, responsible and dependable.

They are extremely hardworking and persevering, so are often in leadership positions.

They are practical and focused on their goals, and appreciate the same qualities in others.

Capricorn Moons are conventional and aren't interested in diverging from what tradition and society expect.

They can sometimes worry too much about what others will think, or misjudge people because of their appearance, causing them to miss out on experiences and inner growth.

They need to learn to see the beauty in difference and be a little less judgemental.

They are most compatible with Taurus, Cancer, Virgo and fellow Capricorn Moons.

The Moon in Capricorn is the best time for magical workings involving work, mental health, relationships with authority figures, perseverance and discipline.

the MOON in AQUARIUS

Aquarius Moons are honest, compassionate and unconventional who don't mind being perceived as weird.

They care deeply about local and global issues and often participate in protests.

They believe it is their duty to do everything they can to leave the world a better place than they found it. Even as children, they often stand up to bullies to defend others.

Aquarius Moons are far-sighted, practical, and if allowed to pursue their passion, can turn out to be visionaries. They love giving advice to their many friends.

They find it easy to make new acquaintances, but may need to learn how to discern true friends they can trust with anything.

They adjust to any situation easily and are not afraid to change their opinions when proven wrong.

They need their personal space and can't withstand suffocating situations.

They are most compatible with Aries, Gemini, Leo and Libra Moons.

The Moon in Aquarius is the best time for magical workings involving freedom, self-confidence, finding oneself, relationships and creative projects.

the MOON in PISCES

Pisces Moons are kind, caring, intuitive and gentle. They love romance, showing their emotions and making others feel good, too.

They avoid any kind of conflict, which might turn them into people pleasers – they need to learn how to handle uncomfortable situations and rejection early on.

Pisces Moons are extremely helpful, real team players who also need to learn to say from no time to time.

They do well in psychology and the arts, especially literature, as they are highly empathetic and intuitive. They often have psychic gifts.

Being open-hearted and trusting, they need to recognise that not everyone is like them and that being trustworthy doesn't have to make them gullible.

They are most compatible with Taurus, Cancer and Scorpio Moons.

The Moon in Pisces is the best time for magical workings involving psychic gifts, spirituality, the arts, introspection, and connections in this life and beyond the veil.

CHAPTER 5

MOON MAGIC SPELLS

a BANISHING SPELL

A banishing spell will remove anything or anyone negatively impacting your life.

If, however, you don't want to remove someone *completely* or need to stay in touch, consider casting a binding spell instead.

For negative spirits, suspected hexes or stalking exes, a banishing spell will do just fine.

Banishing spells are best done under the **new moon**, when the Moon is in Scorpio, Aries or Cancer.

These are all highly protective signs, but if you need an especially strong spell, Scorpio and Aries will be the most potent.

For this banishing spell you will need:

- *Bath salts or shower gel containing sea salt*
- *A black or white candle*
- *Pen and paper*
- *A fireproof bowl*

Start by cleaning your living space and taking a cleansing bath.

Soak yourself in a nice tub of hot water with your favourite bath salts, visualising any negative energy seeping out of your body, out of your aura, getting trapped by the salt water.

When you have enjoyed your bath, unplug your tub and visualise everything that doesn't serve you going down the drain.

Take a quick shower to wash off any residue on your body and dry yourself with a nice, soft towel. If you don't have a bath tub, there are shower gels available containing sea salt that you could use as an alternative to soaking in salt.

Dress yourself in freshly washed clothes, go to your altar and define your magic circle – either by marking it with symbolic elements from your altar, drawing a boundary with your finger or a knife, or simply visualising the circle.

Your magic circle will create a sacred space for the ritual and can help focus the magical energy for the spell.

Call any familiars or guides you usually work with and light the candle.

On your paper, write down the name or describe the person or thing you want to banish, then fold the paper in half.

Hold it in your hands and will it to represent the influence of whatever is written on it. Pick it up at one of the edges and hold it into the flame of the candle.

Taking care not to burn yourself, let the paper catch fire, then drop it into your fireproof bowl.

When the paper is consumed, flush the ashes down the toilet. Wash out the bowl and let the candle burn down.

Your spell is complete; you can thank your guides and undo your magic circle by visualising the energy leaving the circle or breaking the boundary by drawing through it or moving items.

Repeat the spell as you feel it's needed, but if the same presence comes back over and over, consider doing a binding spell first, to stop them from reaching you at all.

a BINDING, or FREEZING SPELL

There are many types of **binding** (restricting) and **freezing** (immobilizing) spells. The spell described here is designed to prevent a person from being able to affect you, without violating their free will.

The intention is for their actions to return to them, forcing them to deal with their own issues without them affecting you any longer.

Binding spells are best performed when the **new moon** is in Aries or Scorpio, but it's worth using any new moon or waning moon phase.

For this spell you will need:

- *Pen and paper*
- *Thread or twine, preferably black but white is fine too*
- *Candle wax*

Write the name of the person or thing that is affecting you on your paper. If you don't have a name, describe them in as much detail as you can.

Tightly roll up the paper: the circular shape will return their energy to them without allowing it escape and reach you.

Now take your thread and wrap it around the roll of paper – at least three times, but as many times as feels right to you.

Tie three knots at the end and seal it with wax from a molten candle.

Take this token and bury it far from your house, in a place that doesn't mean anything to you and where it won't be disturbed.

Alternatively, drop it in a jar, fill it up with water and vinegar, close the lid and pop it in the freezer for extra impact.

Don't forget to discard of it when it has served its purpose.

a SELF-CARE SPELL

Self-care spells are best performed under the waxing crescent when the Moon is in Taurus, Cancer and Virgo.

This spell should then be performed every day until the **full moon** – for at least seven days.

Identify the change that you would like to make in your life that serves your purpose and build the spell around that.

This spell here is aimed at helping you eat healthier, but please feel free to modify it for whatever you want the spell to do for you.

For example, if your goal is to do more exercise, your offering could be a sports item; or for carving out time for yourself, an item that represents a hobby of yours, like a paint brush, crochet hook, or even a TV remote.

be creative!

For this spell you will need:

- ☾ *Two plates and your offerings*
- ☾ *A white candle*

Every day for the next seven days, you will prepare something healthy to eat and get rid of something you want to reduce or remove from your diet.

You don't have to make a complicated three course meal. You can start off with a nice salad instead of a bag of crisps, or even a glass of water in place of a fizzy drink.

Sitting in your magic circle, light your candle and place two plates on your altar: one on the right for "good food" to come in and one on the left for "bad food" to go out.

Start easy: place a glass of clean water on the right plate and place a can of soda on the left.

Say:

"I offer these items to you,
my guides,

Take my cravings, dispose
this vice,

Enjoy this healthy item with me

So it is and so mote it be."

Drink the water and leave the soda on the left plate.

Snuff out the candle and undo the circle. Repeat this every day until the **full moon**.

A few, no-cooking ideas for your offerings could be:

- *A bag of crisps and an apple*
- *A spoonful of sugar and a banana*
- *A box of cookies and a salad box*

You don't have to radically change your diet during this week – easy does it. Don't worry about still eating empty calories or too much sugar.

The main thing is that you keep working on it.

remember:

Always ask your doctor before making any big changes and make sure you have a balanced diet.

On the day of the **full moon**, prepare a healthy meal, from scratch.

A simple stew will suffice, or even roasted vegetables; don't overthink it.

Sitting in your circle, offer this meal to your guides and say thank you to them for supporting you through this spell.

Look at the items on your other plate. Acknowledge them and the reason they are there.

Maybe they are a trauma response. Maybe they are a cultural tradition. Maybe they creeped into your diet to combat a sense of emptiness.

Whatever the reason, don't shame yourself. Be grateful for these items and let them go.

Dispose of them responsibly. Sprinkle some moon water on them so they don't retain any residual energy from the spell.

Bag up all suitable, long-life items for the local food bank and dispose of the rest in the bin.

Now eat your healthy meal and express your gratitude to your guides and to yourself for making it so far.

A closing thought, whatever your goal is: continue making small changes until you reach it.

You can absolutely do this.

You ARE doing this.

I am so proud of you.

a SPELL for PSYCHIC DEVELOPMENT

Psychic development spells are best done during the **full moon** in Scorpio or Pisces, but any full moon will work.

You can adjust this base spell to your needs, according to what you want to learn, improve or receive.

For this spell you will need:

- *Moon water*
- *Crystals: clear quartz, moonstone and labradorite*

Draw your magic circle and use moon water to cleanse your space.

Cupping the crystals between your hands, close your eyes and ground yourself. Visualise a string of energy extending from your spine down towards the centre of the Earth, into its core.

Now visualise Earth's energy travelling up through that string and activating your chakras one by one.

Imagine your chakras as colourful lotus flowers opening up and gently spinning as the energy from the Earth's core touches them.

The red lotus of the base chakra, the orange lotus of the sacral chakra, the yellow lotus of the solar plexus chakra, the pink lotus of the heart chakra, the turquoise lotus of the throat chakra, the indigo lotus of the third eye chakra and finally, the white lotus of the crown chakra – all are open and gently spinning, energy freely flowing through them.

Hold the three crystals in your left hand. Dab the ring finger on your right hand into the moon water and anoint the crystals. Clear quartz for clarity and protection; moonstone for increased intuition; labradorite for increased psychic powers.

State their purpose out loud and apply a new drop of water to each three. Then, dab your finger into the moon water again and anoint your closed eyelids.

Now call on any spirits you are working with and let them know your plea. Make it as specific as you can: do you want prophetic dreams, a better intuition, or clairvoyance?

Set your intention and ask for it to be granted tonight. Don't be alarmed if you feel pressure on your crown or third eye chakra, this is due to the unusual amount of energy that is travelling through them right now. It should stabilise within a couple of days.

When you are done, close yourself down by imagining the core's energy gently leaving your body the way it came, through all the chakras one by one.

The flowers close up and the energy travels back into the Earth's core, taking any blocks or negative influences with it.

Undo your magic circle, then take the crystals and place them under your pillow in a triangle shape.

Let the clear quartz and moonstone form the base and the labradorite the top of the triangle.

Now go to sleep and take note of anything that you experience: strange dreams, shapes, colours, voices – psychic gifts can take many forms.

In the morning, look up the meaning of anything that you saw or felt and consult an experienced psychic about any questions or worries you have.

Never forget to shield and ask for protection from your guides.

Developing these skills can take a while and requires a lot of practice. Don't be disappointed if you don't feel a significant change straight away.

You have started the change, now work on it and see it come to fruition.

CHAPTER 6

MOON ASTROLOGY in EVERYDAY LIFE

This chapter is concerned with how the Moon's placement in each zodiac sign can affect different domains.

We must also always consider the impact of the Moon's phases on anything you are doing.

For example, buying new furniture and redecorating is best done in the waxing phase, while spring cleaning and getting rid of old stuff you don't use anymore is best suited for the waning phase, specifically when the Moon is in Taurus.

SUCCESS in BUSINESS

The best time for business is when the Moon is in Gemini or Scorpio. The Moon in Gemini rules the domain of communication, ensuring that our efforts in networking, information gathering, forging business collaborations and marketing pay off.

It is especially beneficial in trading, building partnerships, redecorating your business space and in anything to do with communication, like ad campaigns, memos, meetings, conferences or proposals.

The Moon in Scorpio, ruling the domain of strategic and logical thinking, ensures that the combination of meticulous planning, go-getter energy and listening to your gut brings success.

It is especially beneficial for problem solving, finding gaps in the market and capitalising on them, and signing new contracts – especially those related to business.

When dealing with business matters, be careful not to be too optimistic and trusting when the Moon is in Pisces and of rushing and not paying enough attention to detail when the Moon is in Sagittarius.

Keeping these times in mind will help you avoid making unwise business decisions and mistakes.

SUCCESS in the GARDEN

Farmers all around the world understand that the Moon can influence the degree to which their hard work pays off.

There are many studies and experiments that explore the link between farming and lunar cycles. Keeping this connection in mind can yield positive results, whether you grow crops for a living or simlpy want to plant a couple of flowers and bushes in your back garden.

That said, always follow the care guide of the specific plant and make sure they are handled according to their individual needs. You can't plant a tropical flower in the tundra and expect it to thrive, even if you have done so under the relevant moon sign.

When it comes to the garden, the signs are categorised according to fertility – how well plants will get established and grow under them – rather than having specific qualities.

The four categories of the Moon's zodiacs

- ☾ Fertile signs: Cancer, Scorpio and Pisces
- ☾ Semi-fertile signs: Taurus, Libra and Capricorn
- ☾ Semi-infertile signs: Aries, Sagittarius and Aquarius
- ☾ Infertile signs: Gemini, Leo and Virgo

Preparing your garden is best done during the **waning moon** in an infertile or semi-infertile sign, otherwise alongside your plants, weeds will grow fast, too.

Weeding your garden is best done during the **waning moon** in an infertile sign, to maximise the length of time until you have to repeat this task.

Planting annuals is best done in the first quarter of the **waning moon** in a fertile sign, because this period will see moisture come to the surface, allowing plants to grow, flower and bring fruit within the relatively short time frame they have.

This also means that root growth will be slower, making our job easier when it comes to removing these plants at the end of their season as a result of their shallower roots.

Planting perennials is best done in the first quarter of the **waning moon** in a fertile or semi-fertile sign.

It may sound counter-intuitive to use the waning phase, but we need these plants to grow strong roots and establish themselves well before growing and flowering.

Planting during this time period ensures that plants have the time and energy to do so.

REPOTTING

Repotting plants is best done during the **waning moon** in a fertile sign, to ensure the plant takes advantage of its bigger, better environment before further growth.

COLLECTING SEEDS

Collecting seeds is best done during the **full moon** in infertile or semi-infertile signs, so the seeds can hibernate until they are planted and will have the resources to grow well.

HARVESTING

Harvesting is best done during the **waning moon** in infertile and semi-infertile signs, so that the crop keeps fresh for as long as possible.

SUCCESS in HEALTH

The Moon can greatly support the work you do to keep your body healthy.

Following the Moon's phases and the zodiac signs it moves through can make healing easier, assist you in losing or gaining weight, and enhancing your appearance.

Remember:

This chapter is not intended to replace medical advice. Always ask your health practitioner before making any changes to your lifestyle.

The **waning moon** is the best time for losing weight and detoxing. Eat lots of fibre and vegetables, especially green leaves.

The **waxing moon** is best for gaining weight and building muscle.

Your metabolism is faster during this period, so you can be a bit more relaxed around what you eat, but don't overdo sugar and processed food.

The **new moon** and **full moon** are especially suited for detoxing and fasting. Always be mindful of your body's capacity to fast and drink a good amount of water.

Starting a lifestyle change is best done during the waning phase of the moon in Fire and Air signs, to move away from old routines and habits, and remove resistance.

Trying for a baby is said to be most successful when the waxing or full moon is in any Water sign.

SUCCESS in ROMANTIC RELATION-SHIPS

Although we can't time when we meet The One, we can try to maximise our potential of a Happily Ever After even by adjusting when we go on dates, choose to become serious with in a partner, move in together, become engaged or get married.

Whatever the occasion, the second quarter of the **waxing moon** is the best time to make big decisions and hit significant milestones in our relationships.

Avoid making any of these decisions around a **full moon**, as emotions are running high at this time and you may end up regretting it later.

The exception to this rule is breaking up and separating. Ending a relationship is best done in a waning crescent phase to minimise resentment and drama.

Breaking up during the waxing phase will increase the chances of a lengthy, nasty separation.

When thinking about significant milestones, they should be timed for when the Moon is in different zodiac signs depending on what you want from that relationship.

EARTH SIGNS

Reaching milestones during the Moon in Earth signs will bring safety and longevity to the relationship, but it will need conscious effort from both sides to spice it up.

The Moon in Taurus brings patience, the Moon in Virgo brings commitment and the Moon in Capricorn brings a strong will to work on the relationship.

FIRE SIGNS

Reaching milestones during the Moon in Fire signs will bring passion, but it will need work from both sides to keep the flame alive yet stop it from burning down their world when things get heated in an argument.

The Moon in Aries brings intense passion, the Moon in Leo brings spicy romance and the Moon in Sagittarius brings adventure into the relationship.

WATER SIGNS

Reaching milestones during the Moon in Water signs will bring care, intimacy and sensuality, but it will need conscious work from both sides to avoid becoming possessive, jealous and co-dependent.

The Moon in Cancer brings devotion, the Moon in Scorpio brings deep connection and the Moon in Pisces brings empathy into the relationship.

AIR SIGNS

Reaching milestones during the Moon in Air signs will bring positivity and happiness to the relationship, but it will need conscious work from both sides to ensure its longevity.

The Moon in Gemini brings joy and whimsiness, the Moon in Libra brings refinement and the Moon in Aquarius brings friendship into the relationship.

☾

May the Moon
bless you on your path
with empathy and
inner wisdom!

☽